This Book Belongs To

....

Welcome to Ayat's Treasure

Coloring is an activity which is perfect to relax and avoid stress. Use your creativity go wild with colors there are no rules. Clear your mind, also while listening to music watching television or just resting. There will be some of the images you will like more and some less, but the most important thing is that you enjoy the activity!

The paper used by Amazon is most suitable for soft colored pencils. If you use them, make sure to keep them sharp so you can get a better result on every detail. You can even take your page out of the book if you want (the pages are NOT perforated, but you can find on Amazon a tool called a page perforator for under US$ 4).

Benefits of This Book:

- Helps relaxing
- Self gratitude
- Develop creativity and imagination.
- Help stay off screen

If you come to an image you don't fee its suitable to be colored in this moment, leave it there, you can pick it again another day! We recommend to practice every day, it helps to be more relaxing each time

If you like this book please consider leaving a review. It certainly helps us grow. Please visit **Ayat's Treasure** for more coloring books.

We hope you have most fun coloring this book, enjoy.

Made in United States
Orlando, FL
30 July 2024

49743450R00030